5 7 9 10 8 6 4

LEARN TO DRAW

Disney
PRINCESS

THE
PRINCESS
AND THE
FROG

Illustrated by Scott Tilley, Olga T. Mosqueda, and The Disney Storybook Artists
Written by Laura Uyeda
Designed by Shelley Baugh
Project Editor: Rebecca J. Razo

Walter Foster

On a balmy New Orleans evening, two girls listen intently to their favorite fairytale about a frog who needs a princess's kiss to become a prince again. Charlotte says she would kiss a frog in a heartbeat if she could marry a prince. But Tiana says she would never kiss a frog! She has other plans.

Tiana's father, James, shares his dream of opening his own restaurant one day with Tiana. He encourages Tiana to wish upon the Evening Star, but he adds that it will take hard work to make her dreams come true.

The years go by, and Tiana works day and night, saving all of her money to open up her father's dream restaurant. And when the fun-loving, carefree Prince Naveen of Maldonia arrives in New Orleans, Charlotte finally sees an opportunity to marry a prince.

However, the evil voodoo man, Dr. Facilier, has his own plans for Naveen and Naveen's disgruntled valet, Lawrence. Facilier promises Lawrence a princely lifestyle and Naveen a chance to live a carefree life. However, with a handshake to seal the deal, Facilier fulfills his promises in a very unexpected and unfortunate way. With the magic of a talisman, he turns the prince into a frog and Lawrence into the form of Naveen. Then Facilier makes another deal with Lawrence: In return for Naveen's good looks and royal status, Lawrence will marry Charlotte and hand over a large percentage of her fortune to him.

Charlotte's father, Eli "Big Daddy" LaBouff, hosts an extravagant masquerade ball at his mansion. During the ball, Charlotte meets "Prince Naveen" (the transformed Lawrence) while Tiana meets and is instantly repulsed by the real Naveen—in his frog form. When Tiana reluctantly kisses Naveen, something unexpected happens…she transforms into a frog herself!

Both frogs flee to the bayou where they meet a trumpet-playing alligator named Louis and a helpful firefly named Ray. Louis and Ray help Tiana and Naveen escape from frog hunters and get to the powerful priestess Mama Odie. They hope Mama Odie can use her good magic to transform them back into humans. During their journey, Naveen teaches Tiana how to have fun, and Tiana teaches Naveen how to work hard. They finally begin to understand and appreciate one another.

Mama Odie explains that knowing what you need is more important than knowing what you want. Tiana fails to understand Mama Odie's important lesson. Naveen, however, starts to understand. As he looks at Tiana, he begins to realize that she is what he truly needs.

Knowing the two frogs have to figure things out for themselves, Mama Odie instructs Naveen to kiss Charlotte, the "princess" of Mardi Gras, before midnight. Then both frogs will become human again.

When Tiana isn't looking, Facilier's evil shadows swoop down and take Naveen prisoner. Facilier needs Naveen to keep his magical talisman working on Lawrence. Naveen manages to escape and climbs to the top of the Mardi Gras float to expose Lawrence and get to Charlotte. Ray snatches up the talisman and takes it to Tiana. But Facilier shows up and steps on Ray. Having run off with the talisman, Tiana is unaware that Ray is hurt. Facilier quickly tracks down Tiana and corners her. He uses his magic to create a mirage of her dream restaurant and her father. Facilier says she can give her daddy everything he ever wanted—all she has to do is hand over the talisman.

"My Daddy never did get what he wanted, but he had what he needed. He had love," Tiana says. She smashes the talisman to the ground. The shadows descend upon Facilier and he vanishes into thin air, never to be seen again.

Naveen promises to marry Charlotte if she kisses him, but she must help Tiana buy the restaurant. Naveen and Tiana confess their love for each other. Upon hearing this, Charlotte agrees to kiss Naveen—not for herself but for Tiana.

But the clock strikes midnight, and it is too late. Charlotte is no longer the "princess" of Mardi Gras, so Naveen and Tiana both remain frogs. But Naveen and Tiana couldn't be happier because they're together and they're in love. Louis shows up carrying a very weak Ray. Everyone huddles around the firefly as his light flickers out for the last time.

Filled with grief, Tiana, Naveen, and Louis take Ray home to the bayou. They place him in a small leaf boat and let him disappear into the mist. Moments later, a new star shines besides the Evening Star. Ray is finally with his Evangeline.

Soon thereafter, the two frogs get married in the bayou, and they kiss. Then, in a swirl of magic, they become human! As soon as Naveen married Tiana, she became a princess—and with her kiss they both became human again.

After their wedding, Tiana and Naveen open up "Tiana's Palace"—Tiana's dream restaurant. The restaurant is everything that Tiana ever wanted, and her true love is everything she ever needed.

Tools and Materials

You'll need only a few simple supplies to create the characters from *The Princess and the Frog*. You may prefer working with a drawing pencil to begin with, and it's always a good idea to have a pencil sharpener and an eraser nearby. When you've finished drawing, you can add color with felt-tip markers, colored pencils, watercolors, or acrylic paint. The choice is yours!

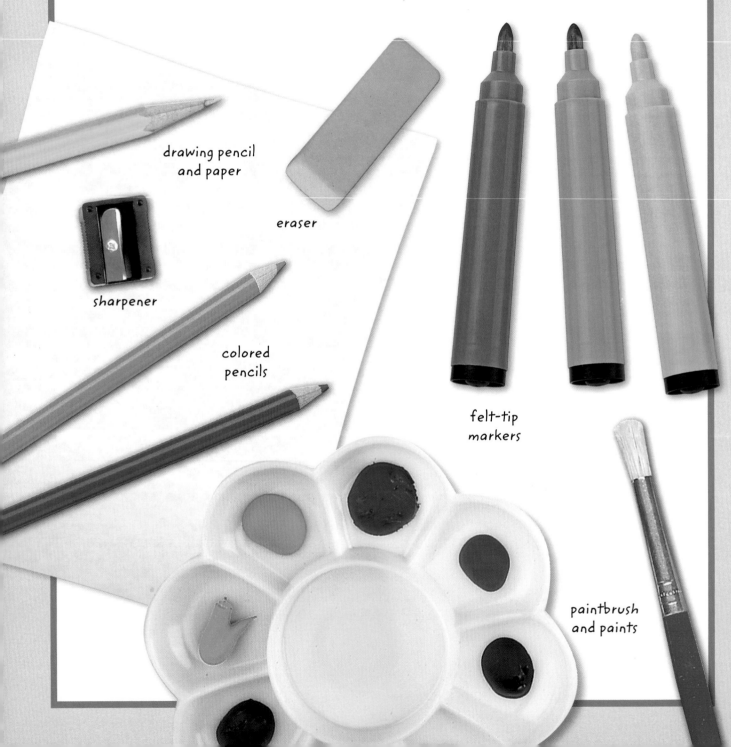

drawing pencil
and paper

eraser

sharpener

colored
pencils

felt-tip
markers

paintbrush
and paints

How to Use This Book

In this book you'll learn how to draw Tiana and all of her friends in just a few simple steps. You'll also get lots of helpful tips and useful information from Disney artists that will help guide you through the drawing process. With a little practice, you'll soon be producing successful drawings of your very own!

First draw the basic shapes using light lines that will be easy to erase.

Each new step is shown in blue, so you'll know what to add next.

Follow the blue lines to draw the details.

Now darken the lines you want to keep, and erase the rest.

Use some magic (or crayons or markers) to add color to your drawing!

Tiana

Even as a child, Tiana is bold and spirited. She makes it quite clear to Charlotte that she would *never* kiss a frog to find her prince charming! Tiana learns from her parents that if she works hard, she can accomplish anything she sets her mind to.

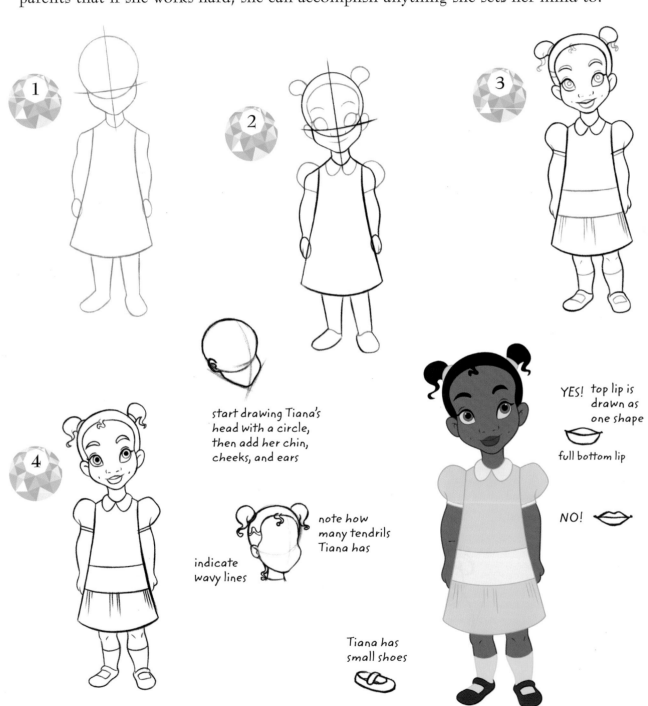

1

2

3

start drawing Tiana's head with a circle, then add her chin, cheeks, and ears

4

note how many tendrils Tiana has

indicate wavy lines

YES! top lip is drawn as one shape

full bottom lip

NO!

Tiana has small shoes

Charlotte

As the richest little girl in New Orleans, Charlotte gets everything her heart desires—dolls, dresses, kittens, and puppies. And she will do just about anything to marry a prince and become a princess…even if it means kissing a frog!

full eyelashes

head shape is carved away from a circle

the nose is based on a triangle

shape of head resembles an upside-down ice cream cone

Eudora

Eudora is Tiana's kind and nurturing mother and the most talented seamstress in New Orleans. When Tiana grows up and juggles multiple jobs, Eudora worries that her daughter is working too hard to achieve her dream. She wants Tiana to find love, be happy, and have a family of her own.

HAIR SHAPES

round
flat
part
round

round flat part
round

YES! eyes should almond shaped

NO! not too round

James

James is Tiana's father who once had a dream of opening his own restaurant. He believed that food not only brings smiles to peoples' faces, it also brings people from all walks of life together. Tiana takes after her father in many ways—she has his strength, warmth, and generosity.

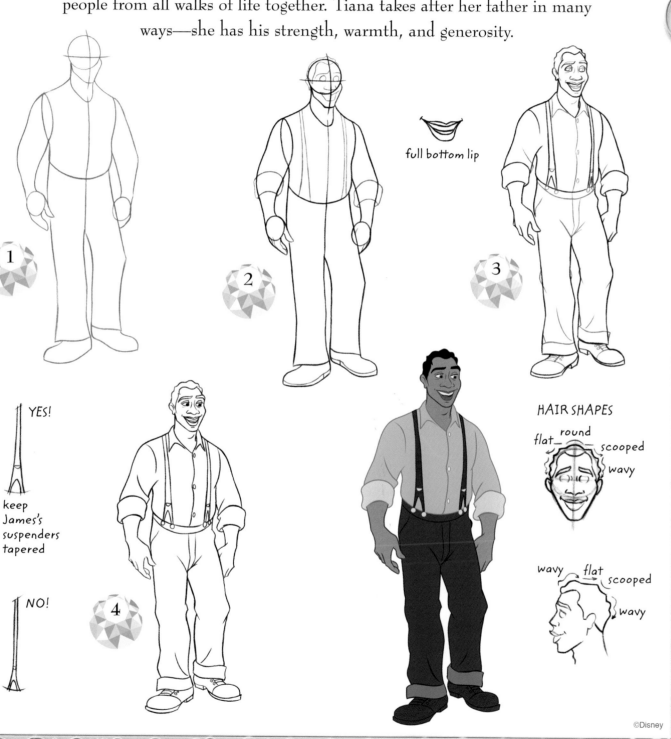

full bottom lip

YES!

keep James's suspenders tapered

NO!

HAIR SHAPES

flat round scooped wavy

wavy flat scooped wavy

1

2

3

4

©Disney

Naveen

Naveen is the handsome, free-spirited, and fun-loving prince from the country of Maldonia. He's a jazz fanatic and has traveled to New Orleans—the birthplace of jazz—to sing, dance, and play to his heart's content. But Naveen's carefree and irresponsible ways have caused his parents to cut him off. Now he's faced with his most dreaded fear: having to work for a living.

YES!   NO!

nose curves out, not in

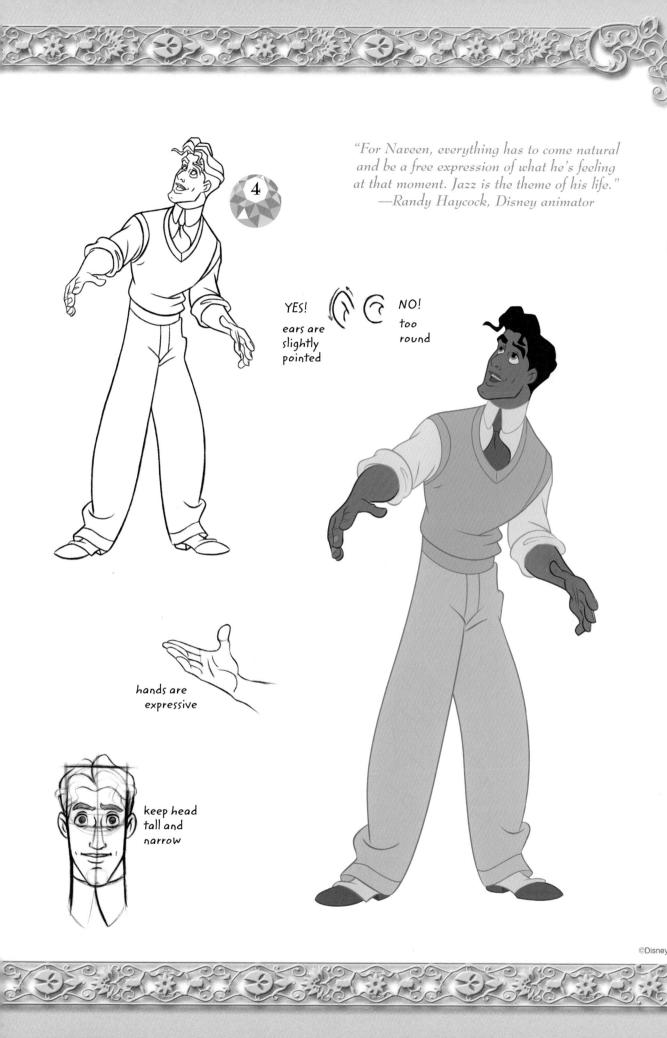

"For Naveen, everything has to come natural and be a free expression of what he's feeling at that moment. Jazz is the theme of his life."
—Randy Haycock, Disney animator

YES!
ears are slightly pointed

NO!
too round

hands are expressive

keep head tall and narrow

©Disney

Lawrence

Lawrence is Naveen's stiff, pompous, roly-poly valet. Though he plays the part of the prince's dutiful manservant, Lawrence is secretly envious of the Prince's charm, good looks, and position.

draw his mouth low on the face

large lower lip

Lawrence's body is pear-shaped

Lawrence's nose is round and upturned

YES!   NO!   NO!

Big Daddy

Big Daddy is Charlotte's father and the wealthiest man in all of Louisiana. Although he is imposing and powerful, he's a big pushover when it comes to Charlotte. Whether it's a new dress for a ball or a prince for a husband, he'll give his daughter anything she wishes for.

ES!

NO!

moustache is full and large, ends point up

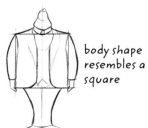

body shape resembles a square

Charlotte

At eighteen, Charlotte is still a spoiled and self-centered southern belle. She only has one thing on her mind: to marry a prince so she can become a real princess! When Prince Naveen arrives in New Orleans, Charlotte spares no expense to make her dream come true.

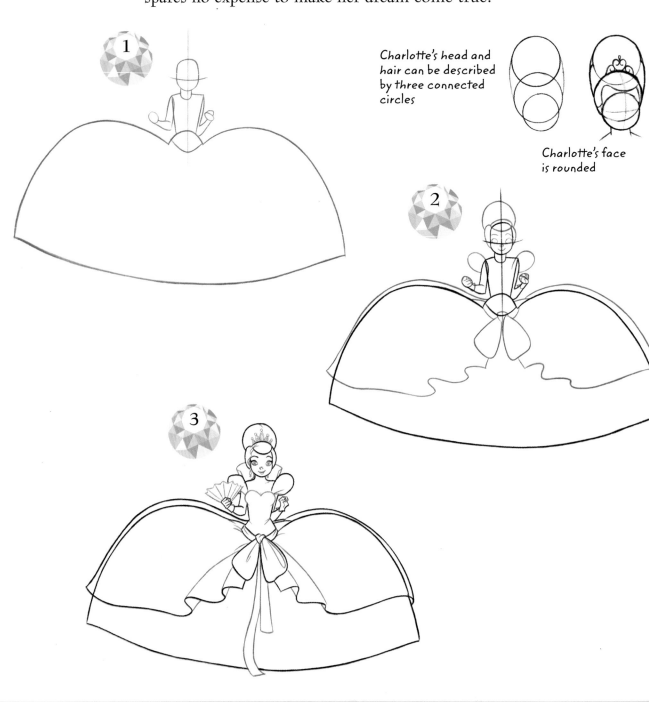

Charlotte's head and hair can be described by three connected circles

Charlotte's face is rounded

4

eyes are large and round,
but the pupil and iris are small

4-5 long lashes

Charlotte uses a fan at
the masquerade ball

*"Design and exaggeration of the
animation is very important.
Drawing, in some ways, is a means
to an end. Whether I want to convey
a certain performance, or I want a
character to look funny or interesting,
I need to draw to get there."*
— Nik Ranieri, Disney animator

Tiana

Tiana grows up to be an intelligent, beautiful, hardworking young woman, and a very talented cook. She works several waitress jobs and saves every penny. Although her friends often invite her out on the town, she always turns them down. Tiana won't stop working until she has enough money to open the restaurant that she and her father had always dreamed of.

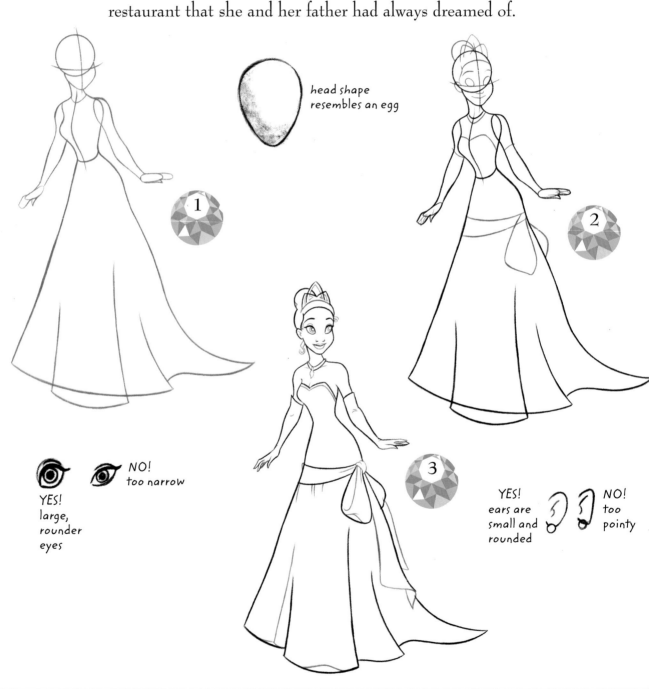

head shape resembles an egg

1

2

YES! large, rounder eyes

NO! too narrow

3

YES! ears are small and rounded

NO! too pointy

"Tiana is the same person throughout. She just literally changes her skin or body. She has similar mannerisms and expressions as a human and as a frog. I never looked at them differently."
—Mark Henn, Disney animator

4

masquerade ball tiara

nose is short and round

rounded chin

Dr. Facilier

Dr. Facilier is a sinister and charismatic man of dark magic who works in the French Quarter. He lures unsuspecting passersby into deals where he promises to give them their heart's desire in return for money. However, when fulfilling those promises, Facilier uses dark magic for his own personal gain. Facilier yearns to expand his small-time business so he can spread darkness and corruption throughout New Orleans…and become fantastically wealthy in the process.

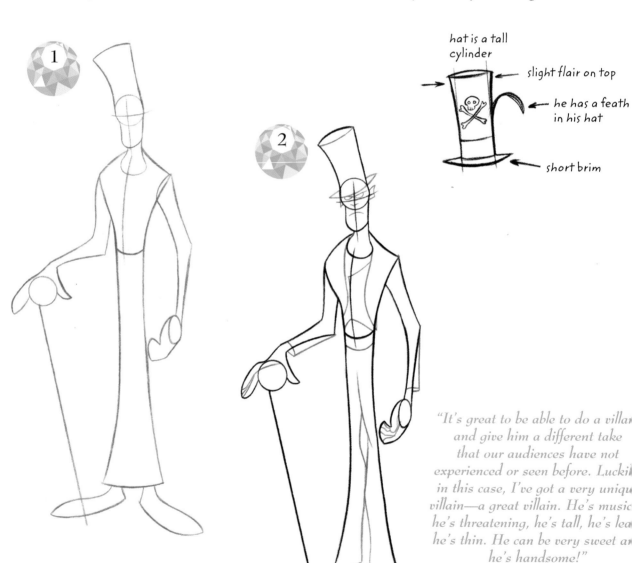

hat is a tall cylinder

slight flair on top

he has a feath
in his hat

short brim

"It's great to be able to do a villa
and give him a different take
that our audiences have not
experienced or seen before. Lucki
in this case, I've got a very uniqu
villain—a great villain. He's music
he's threatening, he's tall, he's lea
he's thin. He can be very sweet a
he's handsome!"
—Bruce Smith, Disney animato

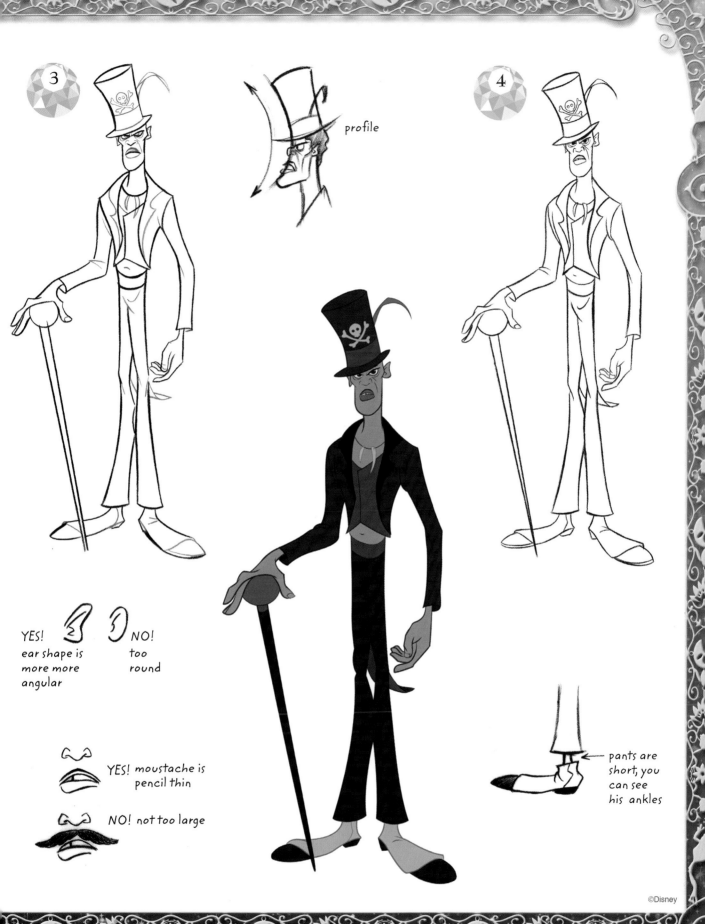

3

profile

4

YES!
ear shape is
more more
angular

NO!
too
round

YES! moustache is
pencil thin

NO! not too large

pants are
short, you
can see
his ankles

©Disney

Tiana the frog

Being green isn't easy! When Tiana is transformed into a frog, she's faced with brand new challenges: finding her way through the bayou, escaping from frog hunters, and catching flies with her long, sticky tongue! But even as a frog, Tiana proves that she's very capable and hardworking. Whether it's making a boat on which to float down the bayou or whipping up a batch of gumbo for her friends, Tiana can get things done.

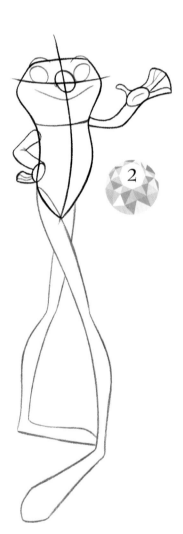

Tiana's eyes are one eye's width apart

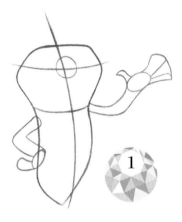

eyebrow

full lashes

eyelid

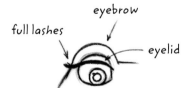

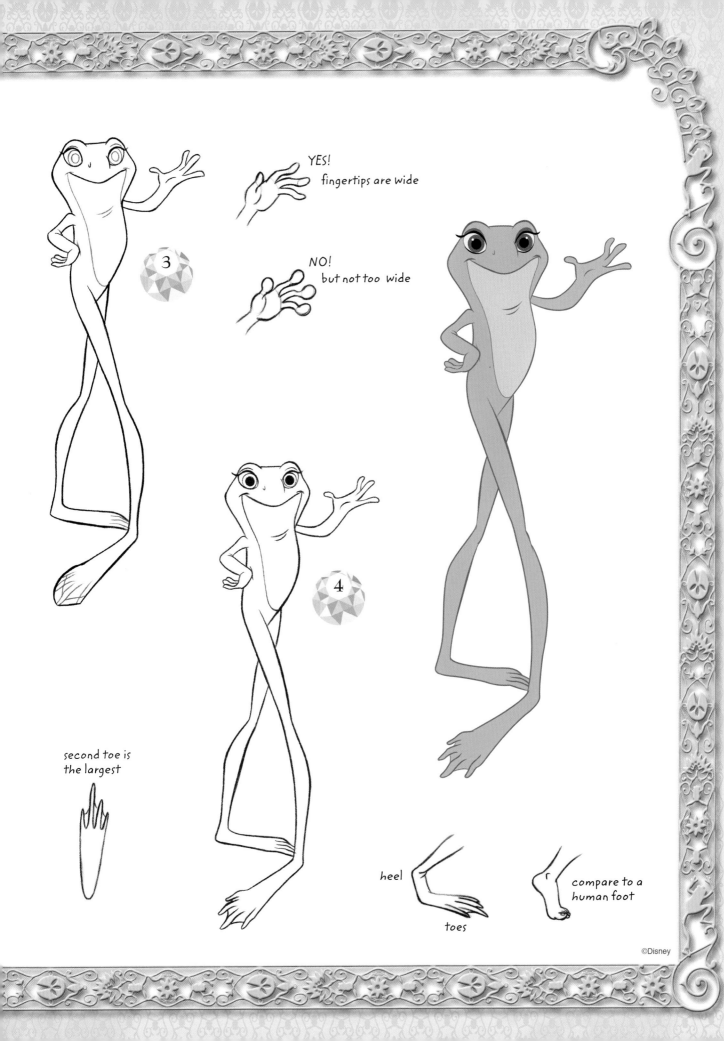

YES!
fingertips are wide

NO!
but not too wide

3

4

second toe is
the largest

heel

toes

compare to a
human foot

©Disney

Naveen the frog

When Facilier uses his talisman to cast a spell on Naveen, the prince transforms into a frog. But even in his new amphibious form, Naveen isn't much different. He floats down the bayou river, lounges about, and plays jazz. But when Tiana teaches him a few things about responsibility and hard work, his views begin to change.

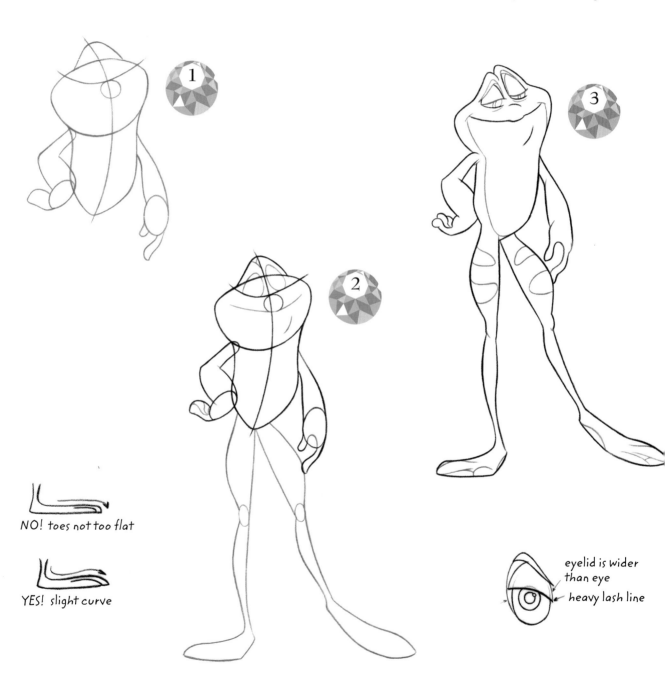

NO! toes not too flat

YES! slight curve

eyelid is wider than eye

heavy lash line

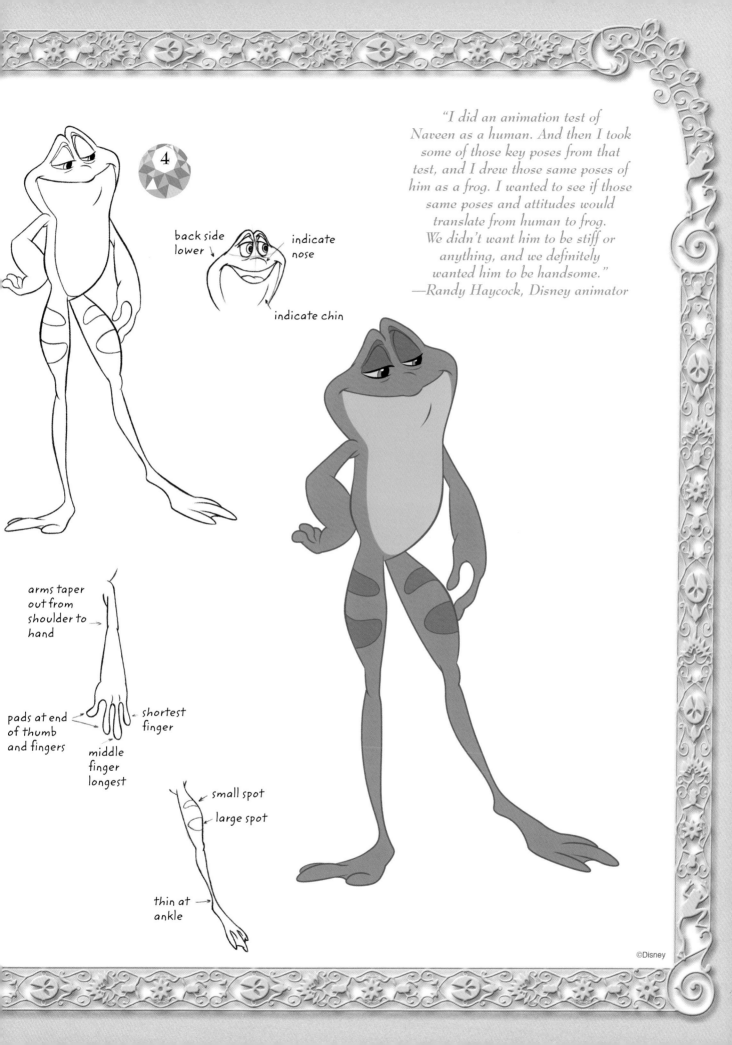

4

back side
lower

indicate
nose

indicate chin

arms taper
out from
shoulder to
hand

pads at end
of thumb
and fingers

shortest
finger

middle
finger
longest

small spot

large spot

thin at
ankle

Louis

Louis is a huge alligator who knows all about jazz, having listened to the great jazz musicians perform on the riverboats passing through the bayou. When he found a discarded trumpet (which he named Giselle), Louis taught himself to play and became a true jazz master himself. His dream is to play for a human audience while not scaring them half to death.

1

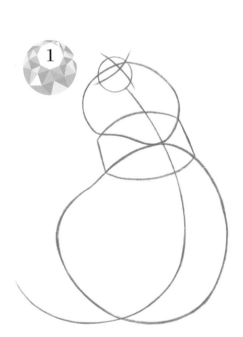

NO!

too round

YES!

show dimension to eyebrow ridges

Louis has tiny hands to contrast with his huge body

draw this shape first

then round out the fingers

2

muzzle should always have "s-curve" shape

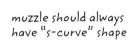

hanging Louis's jaw way back behind his eyes makes him look like an alligator

3

4

pupil can protrude off
the whites

"Louis is generally a bundle of
nerves in a gator suit...however,
Louis has a heart as big as his
girth, which he reveals most
successfully when blowing his
trumpet. Louis's big dream is to
play jazz 'with the big boys' in the
human world. Now, if it weren't
for all those teeth..."
—Eric Goldberg, Disney animator

Ray

Ray is a lovesick Cajun firefly who's constantly pining for his beloved Evangeline—
the Evening Star, whom he believes is a firefly. Even though he and Evangeline are
from separate worlds, Ray believes love conquers all. Someday they will be together.
Ray is also a loyal and courageous friend. He may be small, but he's also mighty!
And he's always there to help his friends when they need him.

*"When drawing Ray, make sure you
have a sense of rhythm. Allow one
shape to flow naturally into the next."*
—Mike Surrey, Disney animator

don't make
chin too round

YES!

NO!

YES!   NO!

antenna shape

3

4

make wing cutouts
asymmetrical

NO!   YES!

keep legs
straighter,
no bend at
knee

Mama Odie and Juju

Mama Odie is a 200-year-old blind priestess who lives deep in the Louisiana bayou with her "seeing-eye snake," Juju. She's a little forgetful and somewhat scatterbrained, but make no mistake: Mama Odie has great powers and is very wise. She befriends Tiana and Naveen and tells them that although they may know what they *want*, they have to discover what they *need*. And only then will they achieve their true dreams.

1

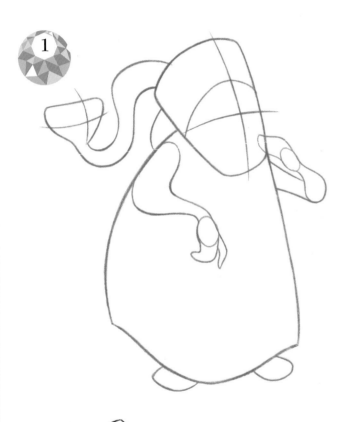

"Mama Odie and her snake, Juju, are truly funny and eccentric. After having animated villains and hero types, I enjoy making audiences laugh with these characters."
—Andrea Deja, Disney animator

2

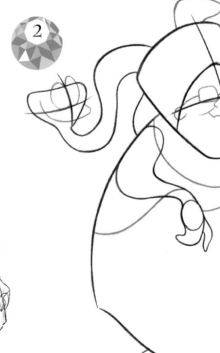

posture is stooped

Mama Odie is 2-1/2 heads tall

3

4

YES! Juju's eyes are two ovals,
pupils are slits

NO!

glasses

YES!   NO!

Princess Tiana

When Tiana marries Naveen, she not only regains her human form, she becomes a princess! Tiana finally gets her dream restaurant and finds true love with her prince!

Tiana has dimples on her cheeks

nose is about same width as the distance between eyes

narrow wrists

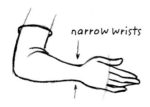

Tiana's bayou wedding crown is made of petals and stamens of varying shapes and sizes.

3

4

full bottom lip

Now that you've learned the secrets to drawing the characters from *The Princess and the Frog*, try creating scenes from the movie or original scenes of your very own. You can draw Tiana and Naveen as frogs twirling about in the moonlit bayou among their firefly friends; Charlotte in her frilly, pink gown getting ready to meet the prince of her dreams at the masquerade ball; Facilier and his shadows lurking about the French Quarter in search of their next victims; or Louis atop a Mardi Gras float playing his trumpet in a jazz band...the possibilities are endless! To create a little magic of your own, all you need is a piece of paper, a pencil, and your imagination!